The Nature Kid's Guide to

CATS

DAVID ANDERSON

LP Media Inc. Publishing
Text copyright © 2026 by LP Media Inc.
All rights reserved.

For information address LP Media Inc. Publishing,
30012 Variolite St NW, Princeton MN 55371
www.lpmedia.org

Publication Data

Cats
The Nature Kid's Guide to Cats — First edition.

Summary: "Learn all about Cats, the Nature Kid Way"
— Provided by publisher.

ISBN: 979-8-89818-203-8

[1. Cats - Non-Fiction] I. Title.

Title: The Nature Kid's Guide to Cats

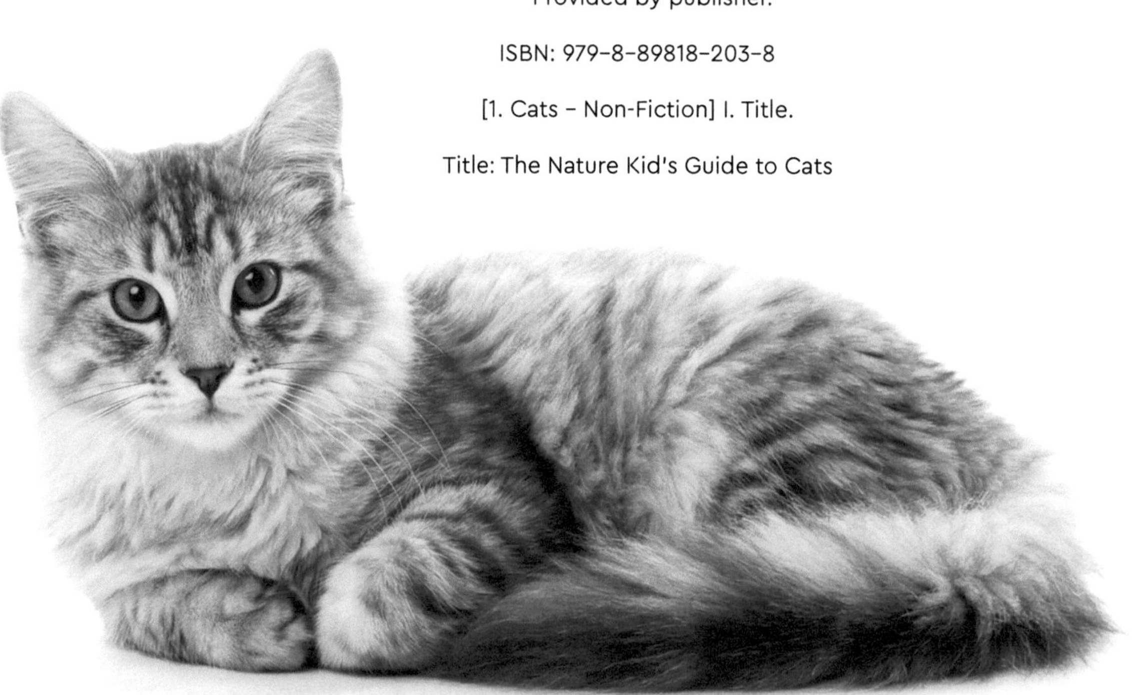

CONTENTS

CATS EVERYWHERE

Purr! A fluffy cat curls right up in its owner's warm lap.

Cats have been our friends for thousands of years. Long ago, the ancient Egyptians loved them so much they treated cats like kings and queens! Today, cats are one of the most popular pets on Earth.

They come in every color you can think of. Some have stripes, some have spots, and some are one solid color. From big fluffy cats to small sleek ones, no two are exactly alike.

Some cats are playful and love to run and jump. Others just want to curl up in your lap and purr. But every cat has one thing in common — once it picks you as its person, you have a friend for life.

WILD COUSINS

A Bengal cat creeps through the grass. It looks like a tiny leopard!

Your pet cat has some pretty famous relatives. Lions, tigers, and leopards are all part of the cat family! They may be much bigger, but they share a lot with the furry friend sleeping on your couch.

Long ago, small wild cats started hanging around human farms. They caught mice that were eating the grain. People loved that, and the cats loved the easy meals. Over time, those wild cats became the tame pets we know today.

Some **breeds** still look like their wild cousins. Bengal cats have spotted coats that make them look like tiny leopards. But do not worry, they are sweet, playful house cats!

SMALL AND SOFT

The longest pet cat ever measured was 48 inches — that is 4 feet from nose to tail!

Thump! A Munchkin cat lands on the floor with a soft thud.

Most pet cats weigh about 8 to 11 pounds. That is about as heavy as a gallon of milk. Pick one up and you will be surprised how solid they feel!

Some cats are tiny. Munchkin cats have very short legs. They sit low to the ground and look quite cute.

Other cats are huge. A Maine Coon can weigh over 20 pounds and stretch 40 inches long. That is longer than a baseball bat! But most cats fit just right in your arms for a cozy cuddle.

COOL CAT BODIES

Swish! A Sphynx cat flicks its long, bald tail slowly back and forth.

Cats have amazing bodies built for hunting. They have sharp claws that slide in and out. Soft paw pads help them walk without a sound.

A cat's tongue feels rough, like sandpaper. Tiny hooks on it help clean their fur and scrape meat off bones. Most cats have thick, soft coats. Except the Sphynx cat, it has almost no fur at all!

Have you ever noticed the flap of loose skin on a cat's belly? It's called their "primordial pouch" and is there for a good reason. It lets a cat stretch out super far when it runs, and twist its body when it jumps. Think of it like wearing stretchy pants instead of tight jeans!

SUPER SENSES

Flick! A Scottish fold cat hears a tiny sound across the room.

Cats have amazing senses. They can see very well in the dark. Their big eyes let in six times more light than human eyes. That is why their eyes seem to glow at night.

A cat's ears can turn in many ways. Scottish Fold cats have ears that bend forward so it looks like they are folded shut! But it does not affect their hearing. Like all cats, they can still hear sounds that humans cannot even hear!

Cats also have great noses. They sniff the air to learn about the world around them. Whiskers help too. If a space is wider than a cat's whiskers, it knows it can squeeze through.

CAT BREEDS

There are more than 70 breeds
of pet cats, but most cats are
lovable mixed breeds!

DID YOU KNOW?

Meow! A sleek Siamese cat calls out in a loud voice.

There are many different cat breeds. Each breed looks and acts a little different. Some are big, some are small, and some have really fluffy fur.

Siamese cats are slim with dark ears and paws. They love to talk and make all kinds of sounds! Persian cats have long, soft fur and flat faces. They are calm and quiet and love to lounge around.

Ragdoll cats go limp when you pick them up. That is how they got their name! Abyssinian cats are the opposite. They are super active and love to climb, jump, and explore every corner of the house. Every breed has something special that makes it unique.

CHOW TIME

Cats cannot taste sweet things at all — their tongues just do not have the right taste buds!

Crunch! A British Shorthair cat eats a bowl of dry cat food.

Cats are **carnivores**. That means they need to eat meat to stay healthy. Unlike dogs, cats cannot live on just vegetables or grains. Meat is what keeps them strong.

Most cats eat dry food, wet food, or a mix of both. Some cats are picky eaters, but British Shorthairs are not. They love meal time and will gobble up just about anything in their bowl!

Fresh water should always be nearby, but most cats do not drink enough on their own. That is one reason wet food is so good for them. It sneaks extra water into every meal!

CLEVER CATS

Some cats can learn to open doors, turn on faucets, and even flush toilets!

Click! A smart Savannah cat taps a bell and gets a yummy treat.

Cats are smarter than most people think. With a little patience and some tasty treats, you can teach a cat to sit, come when called, and even give a high five!

The secret is to keep it fun. Short lessons of just five minutes work best. Savannah cats learn tricks especially fast because they love to play and stay busy. But any cat can learn with enough practice.

The best trainers use a soft voice and a yummy treat. Cats love praise and gentle words. Before you know it, your cat will be showing off tricks for the whole family!

CAT CHAT

DID YOU KNOW?
Adult cats almost never meow at each other — they save that special sound just for people!

Meow! A Maine Coon cat lets its owner know that it wants to play!

Cats talk in many ways. A meow usually means "I want something!" A hiss means "stay away!" And that soft purring sound? That means your cat feels happy and safe.

Cats talk with their bodies too. A tail held high means "I am glad to see you!" Flat ears mean a cat is scared or upset. And if your cat gives you a slow blink, that is its way of saying "I love you!"

Some cats make extra fun sounds. Maine Coons chirp and trill like little birds! Every cat has its own way of talking. The more you watch and listen, the more you will understand.

POUNCE AND PLAY

FUN FACT!

A cat can swat a toy with its paw faster than you can blink, in just one-tenth of a second!

Thwack! A silver Bengal cat bats a ball and sends it across the room.

Playing is important for cats. Chasing, pouncing, and batting at toys keeps them active and sharp.

Cats love anything that moves. A feather on a string, a crinkly ball, or even a crumpled piece of paper can keep a cat busy for hours. Bengal cats are the biggest players of all. They will chase and jump until you are the one who needs a break!

Just ten minutes of play each day keeps a cat healthy and happy. It is also one of the best ways to bond with your cat. Grab a toy and give it a try!

LEAP AND LAND

DID YOU KNOW?

A house cat can run up to 30 miles per hour — that is faster than an Olympic sprinter!

Whoosh! A Savannah cat leaps from the floor to the top of a tall shelf.

Cats are built to move fast. Their powerful back legs work like springs, launching them into the air. A cat can leap up to six times its own body length in a single jump!

Savannah cats are some of the best jumpers of all. They can spring up to eight feet high. That is as tall as a door!

Cats also have an amazing trick. When they fall, they twist their body in mid-air to land on their feet every time. It happens so fast you can barely see it. No wonder cats always seem to stick the landing!

CATNAPS

DID YOU KNOW?
Cats spend about five hours every day just grooming their fur — that is like taking a bath that lasts all morning!

Yawn! A Persian cat stretches out in a sunny spot on the rug.

Cats sleep a lot. Most cats snooze for 12 to 16 hours a day! They take many short naps instead of sleeping all night. That is where the word catnap comes from.

When awake, cats like to **groom** their fur. They lick their paws and rub their face clean. Persian cats spend extra time grooming their long, fluffy coats.

Cats also like a routine. They want to eat, play, and nap at the same times each day. A calm home with a steady schedule makes a happy cat.

FURRY FRIENDS

Bump! A Ragdoll cat pushes its head against another cat to say hi.

Some cats like to live with other cats. They may nap side by side or groom each other. This shows they are good friends who trust each other.

Ragdoll cats love people most of all. They follow their owners from room to room. Some people call them "puppy cats" because of this!

Not every cat wants a buddy, though. Some prefer being the only pet. That is okay. Every cat is different!

Cats rub their cheeks on you to mark you with their scent — they are saying you belong to them!

FINDING MATES

Yowl! A Siamese cat calls out loudly into the dark night air.

A girl cat is called a queen and a boy cat is called a tom. Pretty fancy names for a cat! When cats are ready to have babies, they call out loudly to find a **mate**. Siamese cats are the loudest of all. Their yowl sounds almost like a crying baby!

A mother cat can have up to six kittens at a time, and she can have several litters in a single year. That is a lot of kittens!

That is why most pet cats visit the vet to be spayed or **neutered**. It means they will not have babies. It keeps them healthy and helps make sure every cat has a loving home.

CUTE KITTENS

Squeak! A tiny kitten opens its mouth for its first cry.

Kittens are born tiny and helpless. They weigh only about 3 ounces, lighter than a deck of cards! Their eyes are shut tight. They cannot hear yet either. All they do is sleep and drink milk.

After about two weeks, kittens open their eyes. They start to crawl and explore their world. Scottish Fold kittens are actually born with straight ears that fold over later!

By eight weeks, kittens can run and play. They learn to eat solid food and use the litter box. This is when they are ready to go to a new home.

MAMA CATS

Mew! A mama cat licks her young kitten from head to tail.

Mama cats take great care of their kittens. They keep them warm, clean, and fed. A mother cat hardly leaves her babies in the first few days.

She teaches her kittens how to play and hunt. They watch her and copy what she does. Maine Coon mamas are known for being extra gentle and caring with their little ones.

As kittens grow, the mama cat lets them do more on their own. She slowly shows them how to be brave and explore the world around them.

A mama cat moves her kittens by gently carrying them by their neck!

CAT POWERS

DID YOU KNOW?
Some cats seem to know a storm is coming hours before any person does — scientists think they feel air pressure changes!

Zip! A cat squeezes right through a tiny gap in a wooden fence.

Cats have some cool powers. They can squeeze through any space their head fits through. Their spine bends so they can twist into tight spots.

A cat's purr is more powerful than you think. The tiny vibrations may actually help heal bones! Purring also calms a scared cat down, like a built-in hug that works from the inside.

Most cats hate water, but not Bengals. They love to splash and play in it! Cats can also find their way home from miles away, even in places they have never been. Scientists are still trying to figure out how they do it.

HAPPY CATS

Cats need a scratching post to keep their claws healthy. It also helps them stretch and feel great!

Patter! A British Shorthair is ready for breakfast.

Taking care of a cat is easier than you might think. Cats are clean animals that groom themselves every day. They use a litter box on their own, so there is no need for walks in the rain!

Cats do not need a huge house or a big yard. A sunny window to sit in, a few fun toys, and a cozy spot to sleep is all it takes to make a cat feel at home.

The most important thing a cat needs is you. Spend time with it each day, learn what it likes, and it will reward you with purrs, snuggles, and a friendship that can last 20 years or more.

GLOSSARY

breed
A specific type of cat with its own size, look, and personality.

carnivore
An animal that must eat meat to stay healthy.

groom
To clean and care for fur by licking or brushing.

mate
A partner for having babies.

neuter
A vet visit so a boy cat cannot have babies. For girl cats, this is called spaying.